Dragon Bones and Dinosaur Eggs

Dragon Bones
and
Dinosaur Eggs

A Photobiography of
Explorer Roy Chapman Andrews

By Ann Bausum

Photographs from the
American Museum of Natural History

NATIONAL
GEOGRAPHIC
SOCIETY

WASHINGTON, D. C.

For family near and far—A.B.

The author and the National Geographic Society gratefully acknowledge the assistance of staff members at the American Museum of Natural History and its Special Collections Library, Beloit College Library and Archives, Beloit Historical Society, Beloit Public Library, Logan Museum of Anthropology at Beloit College, George Borup Andrews, and Charles Gallenkamp, author of *Dragon Hunter: Roy Chapman Andrews and the Central Asiatic Expeditions*.

Front jacket: Roy Chapman Andrews led expeditions that discovered *Protoceratops andrewsi*. This specimen is on display at the American Museum of Natural History in New York City. Back jacket: Andrews handles one of the great discoveries of his expeditions—dinosaur eggs. Endpapers: This illustration of a *Velociraptor* skull is from a 1924 American Museum of Natural History journal. Title page: Andrews captured young eagles by climbing out to their nest on an eroded bluff in the Gobi during 1928 fieldwork.

Published by The National Geographic Society

John M. Fahey, Jr., *President and Chief Executive Officer*

Gilbert M. Grosvenor, *Chairman of the Board*

Nina D. Hoffman, *Senior Vice President*

Prepared by The Book Division

William R. Gray, *Vice President and Director*

Charles Kogod, *Assistant Director*

Barbara A. Payne, *Editorial Director and Managing Editor*

David Griffin, *Design Director*

Staff for this book

Nancy Laties Feresten, *Director of Children's Publishing*

Suzanne Patrick Fonda, *Editor*

Jennifer Emmett, *Associate Editor and Project Editor*

Jo H. Tunstall, *Editorial Assistant*

Marianne Koszorus, *Design Director of Children's Publishing*

David Griffin, *Art Director*

Sharon Kocsis Berry, *Illustrations Coordinator*

Carl Mehler, *Director of Maps*

Sean M. Groom, Michelle H. Picard, Tibor G. Tóth, *Map Research and Production*

Deborah E. Patton, *Indexer*

Lewis R. Bassford, *Production Manager*

Vincent P. Ryan, *Manufacturing Manager*

Library of Congress Cataloging-in-Publication Data
Bausum, Ann.
      Dragon bones and dinosaur eggs : a photobiography of explorer Roy Chapman Andrews / Ann Bausum
             p. cm.
      Includes bibliographical references and index.
Summary: A biography of the great explorer-adventurer who discovered huge finds of dinosaur bones in Mongolia, pioneered modern paleontology field research, and became the director of the American Museum of Natural History.
      ISBN 0–7922–7123–8
      1. Andrews, Roy Chapman, 1884–1960 Juvenile literature.
2. Naturalists—United States Biography Juvenile literature. 3. Dinosaurs—Eggs—Juvenile literature.
4. Central Asiatic Expeditions (1921–1930) Pictorial works Juvenile literature. [1. Andrews, Roy Chapman, 1884–1960.
2. Naturalists. 3. Paleontologists.] I. Title.
QH31.A55B38 2000
508'.092—dc21   99-38363

Printed in the United States of America

"In the [first] fifteen years [of fieldwork] I can remember just ten times when I had really narrow escapes from death. Two were from drowning in typhoons, one was when our boat was charged by a wounded whale; once my wife and I were nearly eaten by wild dogs, once we were in great danger from fanatical lama priests; two were close calls when I fell over cliffs, once I was nearly caught by a huge python, and twice I might have been killed by bandits."

Foreword
by George Borup Andrews

WHEN I WAS THREE, my father moved the family to China. We lived at 2 Kung Hsien Hutung, in Peking, in an old Manchu palace. This sprawling 47-room compound was the busy headquarters for my father's expeditions to the Gobi in Mongolia. He was always on the move, engrossed in the big Gobi expeditions or raising money for the next venture of discovery. I saw very little of him during this time.

Not till my teen years did I really get to know this remarkable man. Our relationship grew at Pondwood Farm in the Berkshires of western Connecticut. Pondwood was a plain, no nonsense New England farmhouse, white, four-square, perfect in its way, a total opposite to the great Manchu palace in Peking.

My father needed a quiet place where he could write (now his principal source of income), so he built a log cabin on the edge of the woods some distance from the main house. Much of his quiet time and best writing happened in this cabin, and this is where I remember him most fulfilled, coming to full circle in his life in this quiet, restful place after a lifetime of activity and adventure.

The most shining times for the two of us came each fall when the trees burst into riotous color. The hunting season meant great walks in the woods searching for grouse and woodcock. He gave me my first shotgun and taught me how to do "instinct shooting" at the dodging elusive birds. Also, he taught me how to handle all guns safely. I learned some important lessons of my life from my father: to be self-reliant, always be well-prepared, and to enter boldly into new ventures. He had evolved and mellowed into a patient teacher and caring parent. I was aware, even beyond my youthful hero worship, that here was a most special and important man. ■

The sun casts a hot shadow, but Roy Chapman Andrews is all smiles—he is hunting, finding fossils, and loving every minute of his life as an explorer.

> *"Always there has been an adventure just around the corner—and the world is still full of corners!"*

ALIFETIME OF ADVENTURE began calmly enough for Roy Chapman Andrews when he was born January 26, 1884, in Beloit, Wisconsin. In later years Roy's tale of his birth grew, as his stories sometimes did, to report that he had arrived to a temperature of 30° below zero. During his life Roy experienced plenty of adventures full of enough excitement to thrill any listener, even without embellishment. In fact, when Roy was born, sub-zero weather had recently paused, and Wisconsin was enjoying a January "thaw."

Whatever the weather, Roy was a welcome addition to the large, comfortable home shared by his parents, grandparents, and two-year-old sister, Ethelyn. Twenty-five years earlier, James A. Chapman, Roy's grandfather and namesake, had bought the 14-room house when he moved to southern Wisconsin and its new town on the Rock River.

Roy was born long before radio or airplanes were invented. Electric lights were still a novelty, and most houses did not have indoor toilets yet. Roy arrived to a nation enjoying its first hot dog buns. Henry Ford's original car would not be made for another two decades. Meanwhile, Roy's mother and other American women could not vote and would not gain the right to do so for 36 more years.

AS A VERY YOUNG CHILD Roy would sit on his front steps by the hour, intent on observing birds busy with their nests. When he became a little older, he ventured into the nearby prairies and marshes to observe animals. He enjoyed pets, even wild ones, like a raccoon he captured and tamed. He had a pet crow that would fly after him, cawing all the way, while he walked to school. An avid reader, his favorite book was *Robinson Crusoe*.

From an early age Roy liked to go hunting, and occasionally he was

Roy wore his Sunday best for his eighth birthday portrait.

Roy, first baseman, stands second from right. His class baseball team was school champion.

permitted to shoot his grandfather's heavy muzzle-loading gun. When he was nine, he received his first shotgun from his father. Roy was constantly afoot after that, either with his gun or, on Sundays when the gun was put away, with field glasses and a notebook. He became an excellent marksman as well as an amateur naturalist, cramming journals with notes on every species of bird or mammal in the region.

Thanks to his hunting skills, by his early teens Roy was collecting and preserving specimens of the birds and mammals themselves—standard practice for naturalists of his day. He had taught himself taxidermy, or how to mount animal skins, from a library book. At first he practiced with his own specimens or stuffed the dead pets of his friends—everything from a favorite cat to someone's parrot. Eventually his skills gained wider attention, for taxidermists were uncommon in his area. As he put it later, "every bird and deer head shot within a radius of 50 miles came to me if a sportsman wanted it mounted."

Roy saved the money he made from taxidermy and other jobs, like driving a bakery delivery wagon, to pay for his college education. Roy chose to attend hometown Beloit College, a school known as the "Yale of the West." By living with his family, he kept down expenses.

Roy pursued a broad range of subjects at college, majoring in English. He earned irregular grades, depending on how distracted he became by girls, his fraternity, his baseball team, and outdoor rambling.

During Roy's junior year, a spring boat outing turned tragic. Roy and a young college professor named Montague White, both experienced swimmers and boaters, set out on the rain-swollen Rock River to hunt ducks. Monty accidentally dropped his paddle overboard and, lunging to reach it, upset their unsteady craft. Both men were dumped into the icy floodwaters. Monty began swimming for shore, then suddenly sank from view. Roy, swept in the opposite direction, was unable to help his friend.

Montague White's death in 1905 left Roy devastated but may have led to his later devotion to safety.

After a struggle, Roy finally escaped the current. He rested on a submerged tree limb long enough to restore some circulation and strength in his arms, then he pulled himself ashore. Next he staggered through flooded fields for more than an hour to reach help. Although Roy eventually found safety, Monty did not. When his body was recovered from the river, its twisted shape showed that muscle cramps had seized him before he could swim to shore.

Roy took Monty's death hard. He lost 40 pounds, became easily startled, and shunned being with others. A year passed, and his college career was nearly complete before he regained his former strength, health, and composure. Around this time, he began to slowly lose his hair (he was nearly bald by his mid-30s), and he became afflicted by a lifelong nervous facial twitch. Roy's accident with Monty gave him firsthand experience of the risks of adventure, and it offered him a glimpse at the "lucky star" that he later credited for his many narrow escapes from death.

"Ever since I remember I always intended to be a naturalist and explorer. Nothing else ever had a place in my mind."

Roy at age 20. He credited "many pretty girls" with distracting him from his college studies.

WHEN ROY GRADUATED from Beloit College in 1906, catching the next train to New York made perfect sense. Now 22 years of age, he had recovered from the death of Montague White and looked full of promise—tall, blue-eyed, physically fit, and handsome. Although he had never been farther from home than nearby Chicago, Roy had read about the nation's great museums, and he was sure his dream job was just a train ride away. After all, as a college student Roy had written the director of the American Museum of Natural History (AMNH), in New York City, asking for a job. Roy had been encouraged by his reply to "stop by," if Roy were ever in the city.

Once Roy got to New York, he called on the director. Dr. Hermon C. Bumpus was friendly but firm: There were no job openings at the museum.

"I just want to *work* here," Roy later recalled saying in the interview. "You have to have someone to clean the floors. Couldn't I do that?"

The director was puzzled. "But a man with a college education doesn't want to clean floors!"

"No, not just *any* floors," Roy replied. "But the museum floors are different. I'll clean them and love it, if you'll let me."

Dr. Bumpus was persuaded and gave Roy his first job at the museum, paying him $40 a month. Neither man dreamed then that years later this eager youth would himself become director of the institution.

Perhaps because of his self-taught skills at animal mounting, Andrews

Andrews and another young scientist, aided at times by whalers, extracted every bone from a 50-ton beached whale. Anchor ropes secured it against rough seas.

was assigned to the taxidermy department. In addition to really scrubbing floors, he served as a general assistant, doing jobs like writing labels and mixing clay for models. His responsibilities grew quickly. First he helped taxidermists prepare specimens. Then he collaborated on the design and construction of a 76-foot-long papier-mâché whale model. His next assignment offered an even greater challenge. He and a colleague found themselves knee deep in icy salt water. They had been sent to the shores of Long Island, New York, to extract bones from a beached North Atlantic right whale. Andrews was delighted. He had only worked at the museum for a few months, and already he was on his first expedition!

"I wanted to go everywhere. I would have started on a day's notice for the **North Pole** or the **South**, to the jungle or the desert."

The whale model that Andrews (in foreground) helped construct was displayed at the American Museum of Natural History (AMNH) for nearly 70 years. Two years after work on the model was finished, Andrews was studying whales in Japan when, not for the last time, he thanked his "lucky star" for a near escape. An apparatus lifting a whale carcass broke, sending a 17-ton slab of meat crashing onto the dock. Andrews reacted immediately and dove off the dock to safety. The man next to him hesitated and was crushed to death.

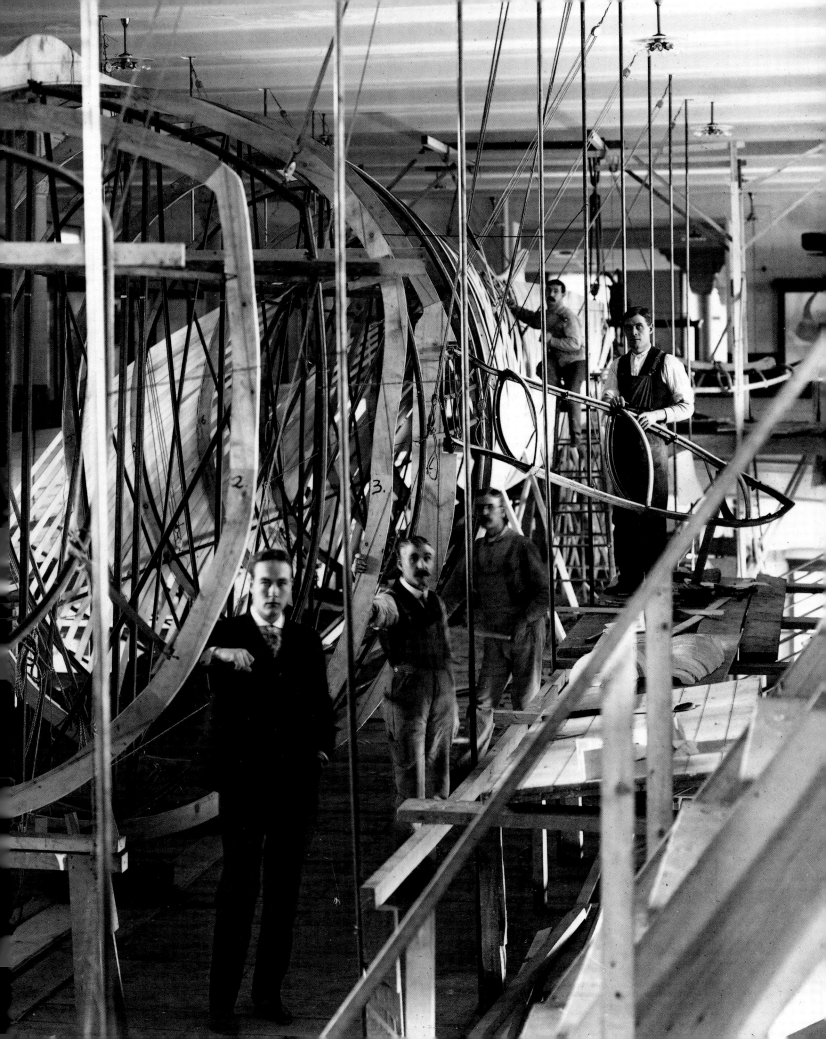

"The lure of new lands, the thrill of the unknown, the desire to know what lay over the next hill! Central Asia was the magnet that drew me irresistibly."

Dr. Bumpus had told the young men as they set out: "Get the whole thing—every bone," but secretly he never expected them to succeed. Andrews and his partner took the museum director at his word. They struggled to cut the bones loose from mountains of flesh. When a storm buried the carcass in sand, they dug their way down to it. Slowly, all but small pelvic bones emerged. Finally, Andrews came up with the idea of fishing for the missing bones in a cauldron of the whale's melting blubber. There they were. After days of struggle, the young scientists had a complete skeleton for the astonished director—and Andrews was permanently relieved of floor-mopping duties.

AFTER THIS INTRODUCTION TO WHALES, Andrews offered to go to the Pacific Northwest without any salary to see what else he could learn about these mammals of the sea. American Museum of Natural History officials consented. Andrews spent the summer of 1908 living at whaling stations on the coasts of Vancouver Island, in Canada, and Alaska. He studied whales while they were hunted and as they were processed on shore. Constant seasickness plagued him on the whaling ships, but he persevered.

Andrews had taught himself photography, and he brought back the first photos ever taken of whales when he returned to the AMNH. He shipped home thousands of pounds of bones, too. In addition, he carried back notebooks filled with measurements and observations that offered some of the earliest facts known about whales. He shared his discoveries through exhibits at the AMNH and articles he wrote, both for scientists and general readers, including his first story for NATIONAL GEOGRAPHIC magazine.

In 1909 Andrews represented the AMNH on a U.S. research cruise in the Southeast Asian islands of Borneo, Indonesia, and the Philippines. When the cruise ended in Japan in 1910, he decided to stay on and study whales.

In 1912 Andrews returned from lengthy research in Korea to find that he was presumed dead. "I have 'died' so frequently since, that I am quite accustomed to it," he later wrote.

His curiosity was so aroused by the region that he persuaded the AMNH to sponsor more research there two years later. Among the species of whales he studied was one called the "devilfish" by Asians. It proved to be identical to the California gray whale. Scientists thought the species was extinct because it had disappeared from North American coastal waters. Now Andrews had "rediscovered" it along the shores of Japan.

When the whaling season ended, Andrews set off on land to explore northern Korean forests. His five-month-long expedition yielded numerous examples of local animals that he gathered from the most remote regions. His isolation from the outside world was so complete that he emerged from

his research thinking he might sail home on the *Titanic*, only to learn it had sunk on its maiden voyage months earlier. Andrews described his Korean explorations in his second article for the NATIONAL GEOGRAPHIC.

Once back in New York, Andrews wrote up his rediscovery of the California gray whale, completing the requirements for a master's degree from Columbia University in the process.

By this time Andrews was becoming known as an explorer. He was not alone. From Robert Peary at the North Pole, to Roald Amundsen and Robert Scott at the South Pole—explorers were crisscrossing the planet in the name of adventure and science. The public loved to hear their tales.

In the days before television and radio, public lectures were a popular form of entertainment, and they gave explorers a way to share their stories. After his first whaling expedition, Andrews signed up to lecture in New York for the department of education. He spoke at neighborhood community centers, giving illustrated talks with his photographs. He became an engaging storyteller, mixing bits of scientific fact with tales of his adventures. Audiences loved it. Soon Andrews was speaking at larger and larger public lecture halls, and his reputation as an explorer—and adventurer—grew.

By 1912 Andrews could tell about swimming in shark-infested waters, surviving mysterious illnesses, being attacked by exotic animals, and sailing in typhoons. Although the stories might grow in size, depending on the audience—much like those of someone who had caught a large fish—they all were based on personal experience. Andrews's scientific successes, combined with his stories about surviving rough living conditions and other hazards, became legend. Today, some say he is the real-life model for Hollywood's daredevil archaeologist Indiana Jones.

Self-taught photographic skills helped Andrews document expeditions like his 1913 study of fur seals in Alaska's Pribilof Islands.

IN THE FALL OF 1914 Roy married Yvette Borup, sister of an explorer who had accompanied Robert Peary on his successful trip to the North Pole. Although Yvette had grown up as a "lady," she was an enthusiastic participant on her husband's next overseas expedition. Their 18-month-long stay in Asia, including nine months in the wilderness of southwestern China, Tibet, and Burma (now Myanmar), was dubbed the couple's honeymoon by the newspapers.

While Roy collected animals, Yvette—an accomplished photographer—took pictures. The pair mixed solid science with plenty of adventure. They emerged from the wilderness with 3,000 specimens for the American Museum of Natural History, along with tales of stalking a man-eating tiger, meeting people who had never seen Westerners before, and falling over a cliff. This time the news that greeted them upon their return to civilization was that some months earlier the United States had entered World War I.

When he returned home, Andrews joined the war effort as an officer with U.S. naval intelligence. Soon he was on his way back to Asia. His knowledge of the region, including several of its languages, was put to active use from a base in China's capital city, called Peking then and Beijing today. His assignments as a foreign spy took him to Siberia, throughout China, and into the neighboring country of Mongolia for the first time. Although he now worked on behalf of the United States government, Andrews could not help but view his tasks through the additional lens of an explorer. In particular, he felt his curiosity aroused by Mongolia, and he vowed to visit it again later as a scientist.

Left: Yvette Borup Andrews, shown feeding baby bears, shared her husband's love for animals and was comfortable either nurturing them or collecting specimens. Above: A public hungry for news of the famous explorer enjoyed this 1921 newspaper photograph of Yvette and the couple's son, George.

AFTER THE WAR Andrews had the opportunity to do just that on a new expedition for the American Museum of Natural History. Roy and Yvette returned to Asia, this time accompanied by their year-old son, George Borup Andrews. They established a residence in Peking. Leaving George at home in the care of servants, Roy, Yvette, and a small expedition party set off for Mongolia to "get a feel for the country." They traveled at first by car and later on horseback, with their equipment hauled along in ox carts.

22

Yvette took photographs of Mongolia when she and her husband explored the area in 1919.
Above: A settlement for lamas, or holy men, fills a broad plain. Left: Andrews rides
carrying an antelope that was probably on its way to becoming that night's dinner.

"I had found my country. The one I had been born to know and love. Somewhere in the depths of that vast, silent desert lay those records of the past that I had come to seek."

> *"There is always something exciting about a map and this was particularly true in those days when a lot of blank areas were still marked 'unexplored.'"*

Roy collected animals, Yvette took photographs, and for adventure they fought off wild dogs. The couple was so uncomfortable sleeping in a bedroom when they returned from the field that they stretched out under the stars in sleeping bags their first night back.

In 1920 Roy and his family returned to New York. Andrews sat down immediately with Henry Fairfield Osborn, the American Museum of Natural History's president, and offered a bold proposal: Let him lead a team of scientists into Mongolia and its vast desert known as the Gobi. Andrews explained how they would travel using motorized vehicles brought by ship from the United States. Supplies, including fuel, would be hauled into the desert on camelback. Andrews predicted he would find a wealth of scientific discoveries, maybe even bones of human ancestors. Years earlier Osborn had suggested that human life originated in Asia. Now Andrews hoped to prove Osborn's theory as part of his research. In addition to fossils, his team would collect examples of living plants and animals, study the geological history of the area, and make maps of it. One trip would not be enough. Andrews estimated it would take multiple trips spread over five years to complete the study at the whopping cost of $250,000.

As details of his plan became known to others, many people thought the famous explorer had finally gone too far. Some noted that, except for one rhinoceros tooth, no fossils had ever been recovered in Mongolia. How did Andrews know there would be more? Others said motor vehicle travel beyond the limited roads in Mongolia sounded risky; after all, it was still a novelty even in the United States. Camel supply caravans seemed fanciful. Expeditions with many experts were a rarity. Everyone agreed that just finding the money to fund the idea sounded impossible.

Andrews admitted it was a tremendous gamble, but at 36 he had a confidence that ultimately made people believe in his plan. The museum director was won over on the condition that Andrews himself raise most of the money required to pay for the research. Andrews accepted the challenge. He toured New York's social circuit seeking donations for his cause. He offered lectures at Carnegie Hall about "The Land of Kublai Khan" and "Frontiers of the Forbidden Land," illustrating his stories with photographs and moving pictures he and Yvette had made in Asia. He wrote articles appealing for help. After more than a year of effort, Andrews raised the required sum.

BY 1921 HE WAS SAILING for Asia to set up headquarters for his Central Asiatic Expeditions in Peking, China. He would be ready to enter the Gobi by the following summer. Yvette traveled with him, bringing along George, now three years old. Andrews rented a former palace to serve as headquarters for the explorations and home for his family. The extensive compound was remodeled to include 47 rooms, 8 courtyards, various laboratories, a movie studio, garages, and stables. Soon other members of the expedition team began to arrive.

Andrews made sure there would be no roughing it at the expeditions' headquarters in Peking. A former palace, staffed by 20 servants, was home for Andrews and his family, as well as other team members and, some years, their families.

Walter Granger, second in command, was a noted paleontologist from the American Museum of Natural History. He had never finished high school; instead his education had come with years of prospecting for fossils in the ancient dinosaur beds of the western United States. Now nearly 50 years old, he was ready to stake his reputation on finding fossils in the Gobi.

Andrews was leader and zoologist for the expedition. Others on the team included two geologists, Charles Berkey and Frederick Morris, who would map and date the layers of exposed rock that held fossils. Also along were a mechanic to service the fleet of desert-going vehicles, professional photographer J. B. Shackelford, and Yvette, who planned to take color photographs during the first stage of the expedition, then return to Peking.

Left: Merin, leader of the camel caravan. Above: Camels, accompanied by the mellow tones of bells, carried every possible supply into the desert and hauled all the fossils out. Team members pulled off soft clumps of camel hair during the summer shedding season to pack around discoveries. Right: Delays and breakdowns—like repairing a broken axle—were inevitable. Chief mechanic McKenzie Young kept the vehicles in repair through every possible challenge.

Local residents who learned of the mission called Andrews and his scientists "the American men of the dragon bones," using the Chinese name for large fossils. Andrews hired people from China and Mongolia to assist with the expedition. Some would act as translators, although Andrews already spoke Chinese and some Mongolian. A few would lead the camel caravan. Others would take care of camp and help excavate fossils.

By the following spring, everyone was busy with final details for the trip. Andrews knew his expedition team would encounter hardships in the desert—sandstorms, temperature extremes, flawed maps, vehicle breakdowns, wild animals, maybe armed bandits or robbers. Andrews planned for all possibilities. He packed everything from fur sleeping bags to spare tires, from medical supplies to pistols and rifles.

On March 21, 1922, the expedition's camel supply caravan set forth from the Chinese border several weeks ahead of the vehicles. The 75 camels were led by a Mongolian named Merin and four other Mongolian camel drivers. Andrews was counting on Merin to pace the caravan so it would be waiting 500 miles inside the Gobi when Andrews arrived at the same spot five weeks later. Each camel carried 400 pounds of cargo. In total, the caravan hauled a summer's worth of food, camping supplies, and ammunition as well as 3,000 gallons of gasoline, 50 gallons of motor oil, and a supply of spare parts.

Andrews planned for Merin's caravan to serve as a sort of mobile market carrying food, gas, and other goods anywhere the explorers traveled. Andrews, his team, and their automobiles would be resupplied whenever they met up with the caravan. Then the automobiles would speed ahead to the next

"Ninety-nine out of every hundred persons think that hardships are an essential part of an explorer's existence. But I don't believe in hardships; they are a great nuisance."

research camp, and the explorers would live off their new stores while Merin's caravan plodded after them. The pattern would continue until changing weather forced everyone back to China in September. If Andrews was right and the Gobi yielded scientific treasures, fossils and animal skins would gradually take the place of supplies used during the explorations, and the camels would return fully loaded.

After a year of preparation in China—and more than two years after the development of the ambitious plan of study—the Central Asiatic Expeditions to the Gobi were getting under way. If fossils were waiting in the desert, Andrews and his team were ready to find them.

The motor expedition set out from Peking on April 17. Within days they had reached the Great Wall of China. This ancient barrier, built to protect China from Mongol invaders, crested tall mountains near China's northern border. The road leading up to the wall was deeply rutted, and the heavily loaded cars swayed as their engines strained to climb it.

A few weeks earlier Merin's camels had passed through the wall's arched gateway and struck off toward the Gobi. Now Andrews and his modern caravan of three cars and two trucks was ready to do the same. As the travelers paused to admire the view, they knew that just reaching this point was a tremendous accomplishment. Now it was time for results.

Tough driving conditions were common in Mongolia and China—the cars encountered everything from quicksand to roads full of rocks and ruts in their typical 3,000-mile driving season.

Andrews and his team take a lunch break in the shadow of the Great Wall. After reaching the summit of the outermost fortification, they could enjoy a panoramic view of Mongolia.

"Before us lay Mongolia . . . a land of mystery,
of paradox and promise!"

"Granger's eyes were shining and he was puffing violently at his pipe. Silently he dug into his pockets and produced a handful of bone fragments. . . ."

WITHIN DAYS they had their first success. Andrews knew from his earlier trips to Mongolia that the Gobi was more than endless sands. Rocky outcrops, ridges, and bluffs were plentiful. Their sedimentary layers were just right for harboring fossilized remains of plant and animal life. Dry desert air helped preserve fossils, and scouring desert winds exposed hints of them to trained eyes.

Although Andrews planned to travel deep into the Gobi before establishing his first long-term base for research, he encouraged study along the way, too. Soon after entering Mongolia, three scientists—Granger, Berkey, and Morris—stayed behind the others to "prospect" for fossils at a bluff of eroding rocks. Andrews and the rest of the team went on ahead to set up the evening camp. Overnight preparations were hardly completed before the carload of excited prospectors roared into camp.

"Well, Roy," announced Walter Granger, "We've done it. The stuff is here. We picked up 50 pounds of bone in an hour."

The next day brought even greater success—the first dinosaur bones ever found in eastern Asia. Andrews was right. Mongolia was not a wasteland of sand. It had harbored great life millions of years ago, and fossils remained to tell the story. Now it was only a matter of time and hard work before Andrews and his team of scientists would find them and reveal their secrets.

The more than 11,000-mile journey from excavation site to the AMNH lab began with Chinese laborers carrying fossils from the field.

Both automobile and camel caravans traveled under the protection of the United States flag, showing that a foreign government would be angry if harm befell its citizens. Andrews knew rebels and bandits might not care and kept up his guard. Left: Flag from 1925.

WHILE MERIN'S CAMEL caravan plodded deliberately toward its first meeting spot at a pace of about 10 miles a day, Andrews traveled more rapidly, averaging 20 miles an hour. The scientists stopped along the way to work, knowing they had plenty of time to explore while the caravan kept moving.

Andrews trapped and hunted animals for the museum's collections. Berkey and Morris made maps of the area's rocks and identified the locations of their camps using stars. Granger, assisted by the Chinese staff, collected fossils, carefully wrapping them in plaster bandages to protect them for the long journey out of the desert and back to the United States.

Shackelford took pictures of the work and of the land and nomads they encountered. Everyone, from Andrews to Shackelford, from the mechanic to the Chinese cook, took an interest in finding fossils. Sometimes the team split into smaller groups and explored separate areas; often they traveled and worked together.

Soon Andrews and his Central Asiatic Expeditions team had traveled 500 miles into the desert, almost to the limit reached by the few cars that had ventured into Mongolia in the past. If their rendezvous with Merin's caravan worked out, Andrews planned to enter countryside visited only by roaming Mongolian herdsmen and their families. When his team found an area that merited longer study, he hoped to stay there for days, even weeks.

As the expedition approached the meeting point, Andrews spotted an American flag flying among camels resting beside the road. Merin, true to his word, had arrived on schedule, just an hour before Andrews. Their reunion was an incredible feat of careful planning, hard work, and good luck.

Merin's camels brought supplies, folding tables and chairs, camp cots, a Victrola, food treats, fresh clothes, even a tin oven that the cook, Liu, promptly filled with a wild goose. Suddenly a roaring cloud of yellow sand descended upon the camp. Everyone sought cover from the stinging grit as they heard the ripping of their blue canvas tents. Camp gear clattered away on the wind. Finally the wave of noise moved on; the sandstorm was over. Liu spotted his oven upended and filled with sand. "The goose, the goose is spoiled!" he wailed, as everyone worked to return order to the camp.

One of the responsibilities Andrews bore as expedition leader was to see that scientific work was not needlessly disrupted by natural and human challenges. The end results of the five expeditions he led between 1922 and 1930 serve as proof that he did his job well. Science was not waylaid by mishap or disaster. He and the other explorers found literally tons of new scientific material over the years. However, his skills as a planner and leader would be tested over and over again along the way.

SANDSTORMS WERE A FREQUENT annoyance. One left car windshields so scratched they had to be removed. Another literally tore Andrews's pajama top from his back. In 1923 a sandstorm surprised the explorers while many of them were at work beyond camp. Andrews and others slowly groped homeward until they found shelter in their tents. An hour later the winds suddenly ceased, and Walter Granger was found to be missing. Then a desert-colored figure appeared in the distance. It was Granger, smiling broadly. He had rushed to mark an excavation site when he saw the storm approach. Then he had guarded the spot, protecting his

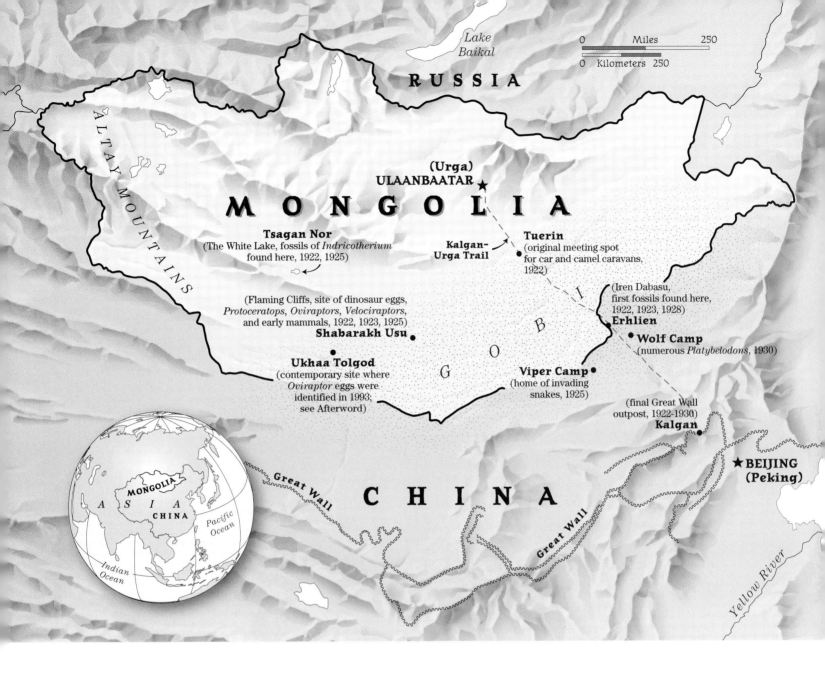

The map shows:

RUSSIA

Lake Baikal

Miles 0 — 250
Kilometers 0 — 250

ALTAY MOUNTAINS

M O N G O L I A

(Urga) ULAANBAATAR ★

Tsagan Nor
(The White Lake, fossils of *Indricotherium* found here, 1922, 1925)

Kalgan-Urga Trail

Tuerin
(original meeting spot for car and camel caravans, 1922)

(Iren Dabasu, first fossils found here, 1922, 1923, 1928)
Erhlien

Wolf Camp
(numerous *Platybelodons*, 1930)

(Flaming Cliffs, site of dinosaur eggs, *Protoceratops*, *Oviraptors*, *Velociraptors*, and early mammals, 1922, 1923, 1925)
Shabarakh Usu

Ukhaa Tolgod
(contemporary site where *Oviraptor* eggs were identified in 1993; see Afterword)

G O B I

Viper Camp
(home of invading snakes, 1925)

(final Great Wall outpost, 1922-1930)
Kalgan

★ **BEIJING** (Peking)

Great Wall

C H I N A

Great Wall

Yellow River

ASIA
MONGOLIA
CHINA
Pacific Ocean
Indian Ocean

face in his coat, until sand collected around him up to his neck.

Not all challenges came from nature. Andrews and his party met every kind of hostile group, from soldiers who refused to recognize official documents, to bandits disguised as soldiers, to undisguised bandits. Andrews, always armed and never intimidated, took the lead as protector of his men.

On one occasion in 1923, Andrews, his car loaded with a late shipment of supplies, spotted a lone sentinel on a rise above the roadway. Suspicious, Andrews removed his revolver and fired two warning shots at the man while continuing to drive. The stranger disappeared. As Andrews reached the top of the hill, he could see three bandits mounted on ponies, blocking the road at the bottom. With characteristic bravado, Andrews dispersed the brigands by charging them full speed in his car.

> *"The snake business got on our nerves a bit and everyone became pretty jumpy. . . . [We] never moved after dark without a flashlight in one hand and a pickax in the other."*

ANDREWS HATED SNAKES. The 1925 expedition team had a particularly unpleasant encounter with them at a place they later named Viper Camp. Andrews and his staff were not overly concerned when they spotted a few poisonous brown pit vipers (relatives of copperheads) during their first day of work at the new location. A change in the weather a few days later, however, made them think again.

The trouble began at night. Norman Lovell, one of the mechanics for the expedition, was resting in bed when he spotted a snake crossing the moonlit opening of his tent. Before standing up, he checked the floor under his bed and discovered a viper wrapped around each cot leg. Fortunately a rock hammer was nearby, and Lovell went to work with it.

Other explorers made similar discoveries at about the same time. Cries came from each tent as occupants battled with invaders. Cool weather was driving the snakes to seek shelter in the warm tents. Expedition members killed 47 snakes that evening with no injuries to people. Although the scientists stayed on at Viper Camp to finish their work, nerves became so frayed that everything began to seem snakelike. Granger hacked a thin shape in half before realizing it was only a pipe cleaner, and Andrews leaped into the air howling after stepping on a snake-size coil of rope.

When it was time to transfer supplies and load up fossil finds, the camel caravan and the explorers camped together.

Merin leads a train of camels across the sand dunes in search of a well. The animals were watered every two days, when possible, but could go as long as five days between drinks. The camels whined, caught colds easily, and spit a foul green spray on anyone who displeased them. Usually they subsisted on scarce desert vegetation, but in 1928 the expedition entered a region so barren the camels had to be fed dried Chinese peas.

Most times at camp were not so adventuresome. Andrews provided well for the staff—comfortable chairs, monogrammed lounging sweaters, records on the Victrola, nutritious food, candles, and, in later years, flashlights for evening light. Each year he shipped from the United States a variety of dried vegetables (tomatoes, carrots, spinach, beets, and onions), fresh potatoes, dried milk and eggs, and coffee. Dried lemon powder was reconstituted into a refreshing drink, and whiskey was shared on birthdays. Andrews hunted regularly, adding fresh antelope meat and game birds to the table.

Occasionally supplies came up short, as they did in 1923 when severe drought slowed the progress of the camel caravan. The scientists made do, waiting at the appointed meeting spot and continuing to work. Andrews hunted more, and the men ate antelope three meals a day. They saved their flour to make paste for preserving fossils. When fossil-bandaging cloth ran out, the men cut up tent flaps, towels, and finally their own clothing—Andrews donated his pajamas—so they could keep working. (The caravan arrived ten days late.)

The safety record for the Central Asiatic Expeditions was remarkable. The most significant injury occurred in 1928 when Andrews accidentally shot himself in the leg while unholstering his gun.

THROUGH LONG SEASONS of work, the men developed a special camaraderie. They cut one another's hair, took photos of each other, and smoked around evening fires made from camel dung, as they talked about each day's finds. Many of them adopted pets: Granger kept two red-billed crows; Shackelford had a pet hedgehog; everyone cared for a German shepherd named Wolf, Connie the vulture, and a baby wild ass.

Andrews's skill as a leader is reflected in the consistent good humor and productivity of his staff. He took pride in the fact that none of his expeditions were marred by quarrels or dissent.

As Andrews and his team bonded through hardships and the monotony

Left: Expedition photographer J.B. Shackelford tamed a hedgehog which he later gave to a New York City zoo. Above: Walter Granger, chief paleontologist, kept pets too. He was particularly fond of a pair of red-billed crows and allowed them to play in the flour paste as he bandaged fossils. They lost this privilege, though, after one of them ate a bone fragment.

of daily life, their efforts were yielding incredible scientific results. Some items they found were obviously important, whereas the significance of others could not be recognized immediately. The focus of their fieldwork was to gather as much material as possible before winter weather ended the season of collecting in Mongolia. Study would come later. Fossils removed from the field were still greatly obscured by fragments of the rocks in which they were found. Their significance might not be fully appreciated until they were cleaned in labs at the American Museum of Natural History or the expeditions' Chinese headquarters.

"In the desert, we had to create our own little world.... Whatever we had, we had to make for ourselves."

Above: One of the Mongol workers used a leftover expedition food container to complete his Asian-style fiddle.
Right: During the 1922 fieldwork season, Andrews received only one letter, an envelope addressed to "Roy Chapman Andrews, Esquire, Anywhere in Mongolia." By 1928 Andrews was arranging for occasional deliveries of mail. His interest here is held by the *Saturday Evening Post*, a magazine that printed a series of his articles about the Central Asiatic Expeditions.

"Almost as though led by an invisible hand [Shackelford] walked straight to a small pinnacle of rock on the top of which rested a white fossil bone."

ONE OF THE TEAM'S most important fossil sites was found by accident in 1922. J. B. Shackelford, wandering off from the idling motor caravan deep in the Gobi came upon a small white skull weathering out of nearby cliffs.

Walter Granger puzzled over the fossil, pronounced it to be something reptilian, and packed it away for shipment to the American Museum of Natural History. Local people called the area Shabarakh Usu, meaning "the place of the muddy water." Andrews, with his usual flair for drama, dubbed the fossil site the "Flaming Cliffs," inspired by the rocks' brilliant glow when struck by light from the rising and setting sun.

Some months later word came back from New York: If you don't go anywhere else next season, you must get back to the Flaming Cliffs. The unknown skull was a new species of dinosaur. It was named *Protoceratops andrewsi* to honor Andrews and his expedition. President Osborn commended their efforts: "You have written a new chapter in the history of life upon the earth," he declared.

By July 1923 the expedition was deep in Mongolian territory, retracing the previous year's car tracks that led to the Flaming Cliffs. Results were almost immediate and more dramatic than anyone could have dreamed. Within days a new assistant in paleontology, George Olsen, made a bold announcement: That morning he had found prehistoric eggs.

Skepticism gave way to excitement as scientists followed him to the site and kneeled around a clutch of eight-inch-long oblong shapes, reddish brown in color. What were they? Could they really be eggs? Andrews had planned for just such an opportunity. Bringing together experts in many fields of study—paleontology, geology, zoology, and so on—made it possible for the scientists to use their combined knowledge to solve mysteries in the field. Now they went to work, each man offering his opinion.

Above: The explorers found so many *Protoceratops* at the Flaming Cliffs that they were able to exhibit skulls from every phase of life, youngest to oldest, once back in New York.
Below: Andrews visited the Flaming Cliffs the first three years of the Central Asiatic Expeditions. Each trip yielded plenty of fossils to haul away.

Finally Granger settled the debate. Andrews recorded Granger's words: "No dinosaur eggs ever have been found, but the reptiles probably did lay eggs. These must be dinosaur eggs. They can't be anything else."

In fact, as early as the 1870s, a few shell fragments found in France had been tentatively identified as coming from dinosaurs. But no one had confirmed the discovery by recovering whole eggs by the nestful. Olsen had found a clutch of eggs so well preserved that they looked like they had been laid just then instead of millions of years earlier. Over the years the Flaming Cliffs became a treasure box for Andrews and his team, revealing numerous skeletons of *Protoceratops*. The scientists concluded that the many eggs they found must be those of *Protoceratops*. When they found the skeleton of another new species of dinosaur nearby, they decided it had been caught in a sudden sandstorm while trying to rob a nest (a theory that lasted for 70 years—see Afterword). They named that species *Oviraptor*, or egg thief. The first examples of *Velociraptor* (meaning speedy thief), were also found at the Flaming Cliffs.

Although Andrews and his team were not finding the human ancestors they had hoped for, they were transforming the understanding of early life in the region. By the end of the 1923 fieldwork, it was clear that five years would not be enough time to explore Mongolia completely—and that meant more money was needed.

Left: Although Andrews made plenty of his own fossil discoveries, Granger frowned on his excavation techniques. Given the chance, Andrews unearthed bones with a pickax and the zeal of a child unwrapping a present. Above: Andrews made the cover of *Time* magazine with a report on the discovery of dinosaur eggs and other new fossils.

ANDREWS RETURNED to America to raise new funds, expand the research, and recruit more staff members. Reporters swarmed over the returning scientists, particularly Andrews. *Time* magazine put him on its cover. Andrews found himself in constant demand by the media, at parties, and on the lecture circuit. A talk by him at the American Museum of Natural History drew 4,000 people in one night. (There were not enough chairs for everyone, so he spoke twice.) As usual on his return from distant lands, he was introduced to something new. This time it was radio—with a live broadcast of the Harvard-Yale football game.

BY 1925 ANDREWS was back in Asia with the largest expedition he ever led to the Gobi: 50 men representing four nations with expertise in seven branches of science, eight vehicles, and a supply caravan with 150 camels. When Andrews returned to New York after this expedition, he raised more money, including $50,000 from lecture fees. He spoke at New York's Carnegie Hall to two sold-out crowds. Andrews wrote more, too. Popular works like the book *On the Trail of Ancient Man* and, later, *Ends of the Earth* added to his growing fame and to public interest in his work.

Civil wars in China forced Andrews to cancel plans for expeditions in 1926 and 1927. In fact, just to be on the safe side, Andrews had machine guns installed on the roof of the Peking headquarters to protect staff members, equipment, and his family. The final Central Asiatic Expeditions took place in 1928 and 1930. On both trips Andrews and his explorers had more trouble than ever from uncooperative Chinese officials, disrespectful soldiers, and bandits. It was clear that the Central Asiatic Expeditions would have to stop, even though more scientific work remained. Asia was becoming increasingly unsafe, and the Great Depression, which had begun the previous fall, made resources scarce. Although they left the field reluctantly, Walter Granger observed: "Well Roy, the Gobi has paid its debt."

IN ALL, ANDREWS LED FIVE expeditions between 1922 and 1930, traveling thousands of miles in Mongolia and China in the process. Although his team never found bones of early humans (Africa, not Asia would prove to be the "birthplace" of human evolution), the final tally of their collections is staggering. Andrews and his explorers identified more than 380 new species of living and fossilized animals and plants. They made detailed notes on

AMNH President Henry Fairfield Osborn had sent Andrews off with the words, "The fossils are there. Go and find them." With every successive expedition, Andrews and his team proved him right.

Andrews and his scientists found more than dinosaurs. They unearthed extinct mammals of all sizes, too. Above: Excavators protect the giant leg bones of an *Indricotherium* with splints before removing it from the field. This extinct beast was twice as tall as a modern elephant. Right: The smallest mammal fossils found came from tiny rodent-like creatures that lived alongside the last dinosaurs.

more than 1,500 additional species and wrote briefly about nearly 7,000 others. They documented their efforts and glimpses of life in the region on 50,000 feet of motion-picture film and thousands of still photographs. Besides dinosaurs and dinosaur eggs, Andrews and his team discovered fossils of a mastodon with a shovel-shaped jaw, tiny early mammals, and a giant rhinoceros-like creature that was the largest land mammal of all time.

Andrews made sure these findings were carefully recorded. His vision of a 12-volume series about his expeditions did not come to pass, but staff members did produce 6 volumes. Andrews wrote most of the 600-plus-page introductory work—*The New Conquest of Central Asia*. Science mixes with adventure as he describes everything from sandstorms to packing lists and from discoveries of bones to battles with bandits in this detailed account of his five expeditions. His third and final NATIONAL GEOGRAPHIC article, an overview of the Central Asiatic Expeditions, was published soon after in 1933.

One casualty of Andrews's extended stay in Asia was his marriage. After 1922 Yvette no longer joined her husband's expeditions. J. B. Shackelford had taken her place as expedition photographer, leaving her without work to do. (Museum officials frowned on bringing idle spouses into the field.) Furthermore, with the birth of their second son, Roy Kevin, in 1924, Yvette had less freedom to travel. These long separations—and others while Andrews went on fund-raising trips to the United States—contributed to irreconcilable differences in their marriage. They were divorced in 1931.

A model shows how the *Platybelodon*, or shovel-tusked mastodon, might have used its jaw to scoop up water plants.

THE FOLLOWING YEAR Andrews vacated the former palace that had served as his headquarters for a dozen years and returned to New York. All efforts to arrange for further fieldwork were fruitless. The political situation in China kept getting worse, and the Great Depression gave no signs of ending. Soon after, Andrews wrote a friend that his "plans are very indefinite because there is no money left in the world as near as I can discover."

"'Never' is a long word but I knew that for the last time my caravan had fought its way across the desolate reaches of the Gobi to this treasure vault of world history."

By 1926 threats from bandits and rival groups of soldiers made many roads in Mongolia and China impassable, forcing Andrews to cancel some expeditions. His 1928 caravan (left) was escorted into the hazardous region by members of the Chinese cavalry. Andrews and his men were heavily armed, too. Such challenges helped end the Central Asiatic Expeditions in 1930.

> "For 25 years I haven't stayed 12 months in any one country. My home has been wherever I make my campfire."

Back in New York, Andrews hobnobbed regularly with other explorers like polar traveler Richard Byrd (seated). Andrews shared a radio show with some and swapped stories with others during regular meetings of the Explorers Club.

In 1934, with no hopes for returning to Asia and no other prospects for fieldwork, Andrews, now 50, agreed to serve as director of the institution where he got his start mopping floors. At the same time he married again, wedding a young widow named Wilhelmina "Billie" Christmas. During the next seven years he sought to expand public interest in the American Museum of Natural History through the development of new exhibit spaces. He oversaw the opening of the Hall of African Mammals, the Hayden Planetarium, and the Hall of North American Mammals.

Even with these successes, Andrews tired of trying to raise money during hard times, and he disliked the inevitable disputes about how to spend limited funds. By the end of 1941, Andrews, now age 57, offered to retire. Trustees of the museum were hopeful that someone else would have better luck managing the strapped institution. They accepted his resignation and named him an honorary director. Thirty-five years of active museum work were over.

Soon after Andrews retired, he and Billie moved full-time to Pondwood Farm, their weekend retreat in Colebrook, Connecticut. There Andrews wrote more extensively than ever, completing his autobiographical *Under a Lucky Star* and sharing the story about his life at the farm with *An Explorer Comes Home*. He wrote for children as well, most notably with *All About Whales, All About Dinosaurs,* and *All About Strange Beasts of the Past.*

In 1934 the whale skeleton Andrews had helped recover from Long Island more than 25 years earlier was finally exhibited at the AMNH. Andrews, by then director of the museum, stood on a ladder before the whale's baleen-filled jaw for this publicity photo.

Andrews had his faults as an explorer, particularly when evaluated by modern standards. Like others of his era, he approached the globe confident of his right to explore any corner of it, viewing his efforts as a sort of scientific conquest. Today, readers cringe at some of his writings and opinions as well as his presumption to claim ownership to unlimited material collected on foreign soil. Andrews did show a greater appreciation than many of his generation for the people he met and worked with in other lands. For example, he helped arrange for two promising Chinese staff members to spend nearly a year in training at the American Museum of

> *"The best museum men and the best explorers are born, not made. . . . Few last very long. There is too much work, which becomes mere drudgery if one's heart is not in it."*

Natural History. Yet once they returned to Asia to work alongside the professional paleontologists, their discoveries and efforts were not recognized to the same extent as those of Western scientists.

MEMORIES OF ASIA remained strong for Andrews. Ten years after ending fieldwork there he wrote of it longingly to an American who had traveled with him in the Gobi: "I often feel very homesick for Mongolia. I am afraid neither of us will ever see it again, but after all we have some wonderful memories." Andrews visited China once after his Central Asiatic Expeditions ended—on a pleasure trip with Billie. But he never reentered Mongolia.

On March 11, 1960, Andrews died from a heart attack in California, where he and Billie had moved a few years earlier. He was 76. Andrews is buried in the Chapman family plot in Beloit with his grandparents, parents, and sister.

Some claimed that the death of Andrews and others of his generation signaled an end to adventurous exploration, but Andrews had predicted otherwise. "To those who imagine that exploration has lost its romance, I may say that the qualities of courage and endurance, the willingness to undergo hardships and to face death, are just as necessary today as they were to the first man who struggled through snow towards the Pole or braved the sandstorms of the desert."

Although Andrews never returned to sandstorms again, he set a standard and blazed a path that others were drawn to follow. "We have shown the way, have broken the trail as it were," he wrote. "Later, others will reap a rich harvest." ■

Andrews and his second wife, Billie, liked to hunt and fish together at Pondwood Farm, their retirement retreat in Connecticut.

Afterword

ROY CHAPMAN ANDREWS continues to influence science and exploration in quiet but important ways. Researchers still study the collections of his Central Asiatic Expeditions. Fossils he found remain on display at the American Museum of Natural History (AMNH). His approach to field research—unique at the time for using a team of many specialists with modern transportation—became the standard for expeditions around the globe. His many books, including *All About Dinosaurs*, helped inspire a new generation of children to become paleontologists.

When Andrews left Mongolia in 1930, he never dreamed 60 years would pass before Americans would be permitted to conduct field research there again. It was not until 1990, following the breakup of the Soviet Union, that Americans were invited back to the Gobi. Michael Novacek, an AMNH paleontologist who grew up reading *All About Dinosaurs*, helped organize the cooperative venture. The first joint research between the AMNH and the Mongolian Academy of Sciences was so successful that Novacek, senior vice president and provost of science at the museum, has helped lead expeditions to the Gobi every year since.

Unlike earlier days, these new expeditions routinely include women scientists. Gone are the long, winding camel caravans. Now Mercedes-Benz jeeps and trucks are resupplied by surplus Soviet military vehicles. Reckoning by the stars has given way to satellite-guided navigation. One thing has not changed: Mongolia remains wild and remote. As a result, adventures and hardships continue, including the inevitable Gobi sandstorms, lost (and later found) expedition members, and so on.

As part of today's cooperative effort, Mongolian scientists visit the AMNH to receive training and curatorial experience unavailable in their country. Important fossils from today's joint expeditions, now being prepared and studied in the United States, will eventually be copied. Casts will remain at the

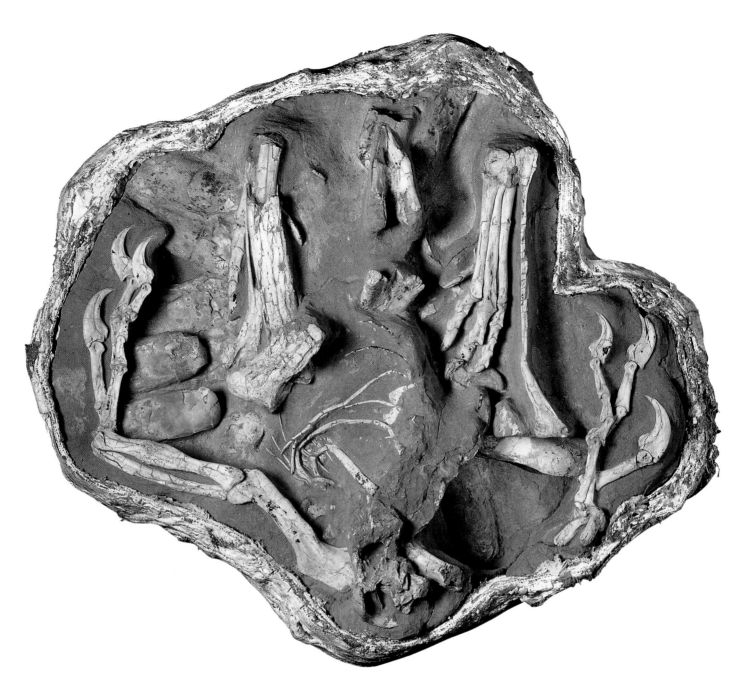

Fossils found during recent Gobi expeditions show that Andrews and his team mislabeled *Oviraptor* when they called it an egg thief. New fossils show their skeletons inside what were formerly thought to be *Protoceratop* eggs. Above: an *Oviraptor* parent nests protectively on top of its eggs.

American Museum of Natural History and the originals will return to Mongolia.

From the beginning in 1990, the Mongolian-AMNH Expeditions have recovered notable fossils. These discoveries enrich the evolving understanding of the dinosaur era and are a reminder that expeditions led by Andrews were only the beginning of a continuing inquiry into the natural history of the Gobi. No doubt further secrets from the past still lie hidden in remote areas of Mongolia, waiting to be found by any team of explorers with the vision, talent, and courage to seek them. ■

Chronology

Medals Andrews earned include (left to right): Charles P. Daly Medal, Explorers Club Medal, Hungarian Geographic Society Medal, and National Geographic Society Hubbard Medal.

1884 Born in Beloit, Wisconsin, on January 26

1906 Graduates from Beloit College and joins staff of American Museum of Natural History, New York City

1908 Conducts first field research studying whales along Alaskan and Canadian coasts; publishes first scientific paper; enters Columbia University as a graduate student while working at the AMNH

1909 Conducts research among Southeast Asian islands

1910 Studies whales in Japan

1912 "Rediscovers" California gray whale in Japanese waters; conducts his first Asian land research by exploring remote areas of northern Korea

1913 Earns masters degree from Columbia University with dissertation on the California gray whale

1914 Marries Yvette Borup

1916-17 Fieldwork in China, Tibet, and Burma with Yvette

1917 George Borup Andrews born on December 26

1918 Does naval intelligence work in Asia during World War I; visits Mongolia for the first time

1919 Conducts first fieldwork in Mongolia with Yvette

1922 With his team of explorers, departs Chinese headquarters by motor caravan on April 17, heading for the Gobi in Mongolia

1923 Discovers dinosaur eggs in the Gobi on July 13 during second expedition to Mongolia

1924 Roy Kevin Andrews born on January 20

1925 Largest expedition to Mongolia

1928 Returns to the Gobi after delays due to civil wars

1930 Final Central Asiatic Expedition

1931 Divorced from Yvette; awarded Hubbard Medal by National Geographic Society

1932 Closes headquarters of Central Asiatic Expeditions in Peking and returns to New York

1934 Named director of the American Museum of Natural History

1935 Marries Wilhelmina "Billie" Christmas on February 21

1941 Resigns as director of American Museum of Natural History effective January 1, 1942

1960 Dies of a heart attack on March 11; buried in Beloit, Wisconsin

Resource Guide

Quotes from Roy Chapman Andrews are taken from his books, cited below, and from his letters now archived in the American Museum of Natural History's Special Collections Library.

BOOKS

Andrews, Roy Chapman. *Ends of the Earth.* New York: National Travel Club, 1929.

____. *An Explorer Comes Home. New York:* Doubleday & Company, Inc., 1947.

____. *The New Conquest of Central Asia.* Volume One, *Natural History of Central Asia.* New York: The American Museum of Natural History, 1932.

____. *On the Trail of Ancient Man.* New York: G. P. Putnam's Sons, 1926.

____. *Under a Lucky Star.* New York: The Viking Press, 1943.

Novacek, Michael. *Dinosaurs of the Flaming Cliffs.* New York: Anchor Books, Doubleday, 1996.

Preston, Douglas J. *Dinosaurs in the Attic: An Excursion into the American Museum of Natural History.* New York: St. Martin's Press, 1986.

BOOKS WRITTEN ESPECIALLY FOR YOUNG READERS

Andrews, Roy Chapman. *All About Dinosaurs.* New York: Random House, 1953.

Cummings, Pat, and Linda Cummings. *Talking With Adventurers.* "Michael Novacek." Washington, D.C.: National Geographic Society, 1998.

Dingus, Lowell, and Mark A. Norell. *Searching for* Velociraptor. New York: HarperCollins, 1996.

Tanaka, Shelley. *Graveyards of the Dinosaurs.* New York: Hyperion/ Madison Press, 1998.

MAGAZINE ARTICLES

Andrews, Roy Chapman. "Explorations in the Gobi Desert." Accompanied by color photo essay "Nomad Life and Fossil Treasures of Mongolia." NATIONAL GEOGRAPHIC (June 1933) 653–716.

____. "Exploring Unknown Corners of the Hermit Kingdom." NATIONAL GEOGRAPHIC (July 1919) 24–48.

____. "Shore-Whaling: A World Industry." NATIONAL GEOGRAPHIC (May 1911) 411–442.

Webster, Donovan. "Dinosaurs of the Gobi: Unearthing a Fossil Trove." NATIONAL GEOGRAPHIC (July 1996) 40-84.

VIDEOS

"Dinosaurs of the Gobi," *Nova.* Public Broadcasting Service, 1994.

"The Dinosaur Hunters," National Geographic EXPLORER series, 1997.

PLACES TO VISIT

The American Museum of Natural History
Central Park West at 79th St.
New York City, New York
10024 (212) 769-5100
Or travel to the Gobi on the Internet at www. amnh.org/nationalcenter/

Field Museum of Natural History
1400 South Lake Shore Dr.
Chicago, Illinois 60605
(312) 922-9410

The Roy Chapman Andrews Society
c/o Beloit Convention and Visitors Bureau
1003 Pleasant St.
Beloit, Wisconsin 53511
(608) 365-4838 or (800) 423-5648

PICTURE CREDITS

Abbreviations used: American Museum of Natural History: AMNH; James B. Shackelford: JBS; Roy Chapman Andrews: RCA.

Front cover (top) AMNH #312326, (bottom) AMNH #411044; Back cover JBS, AMNH #410764; Endpapers AMNH; p. 1 AMNH #410765; pp. 2-3 JBS, AMNH #410988; p. 5 JBS, AMNH #411044; p. 7 AMNH #258467; p. 9 Courtesy of Beloit Historical Society; pp. 10-11 Courtesy of Beloit College Archives; p. 12 Courtesy of Beloit Historical Society; p. 13 RCA, AMNH #24337; pp. 14-15 J. Otis Wheelock, AMNH #31598; p. 17 RCA, AMNH #219034; pp. 18-19 RCA, AMNH #219142; p. 20 AMNH #228953; p. 21 from *Brooklyn Standard* courtesy of George B. Andrews; p. 22 (bottom) Yvette B. Andrews, AMNH #241737; pp. 22-23 Yvette B. Andrews, AMNH #242013; p. 25 JBS, AMNH #108640; p. 26 (top) JBS, AMNH #110266; p. 26 (below) JBS, AMNH #108687; p. 27 JBS, AMNH #265322; pp. 28-29 JBS, AMNH #282812; pp. 30-31 JBS, AMNH #410957; pp. 32-33 JBS, AMNH #265338; p. 34 (bottom) D. Finnin, AMNH #2A21320; pp. 34-35 JBS, AMNH #410949; pp. 38-39 AMNH #251088; pp. 40-41 JBS, AMNH #410783; p. 42 RCA, AMNH #251457; p. 43 RCA, AMNH #251465; p. 44 (left) RCA, AMNH #251038; pp. 44-45 JBS, AMNH #410926; p. 47 (top), JBS, AMNH #258394; p. 47 (bottom), JBS, AMNH #410767; p. 48 JBS, AMNH #410764; p. 49 Time Life Syndication; pp. 50-51 JBS, AMNH #411042; p. 52 (top) AMNH; p. 52 (bottom) JBS, AMNH #258384; p. 53 Dutcher and Rice, AMNH #117092; pp. 54-55 JBS, AMNH #410904; p. 56 AP/Wide World Photos; p. 57 Julius Kirschner, AMNH #314510; p. 59 Courtesy of George B. Andrews; p. 61 Beckett, AMNH #5789; p. 62 Mark Thiessen, NGP, medals courtesy of George B. Andrews

Index

Photographs are indicated by **boldface.** If photographs are included within a page span, the entire span is boldface.

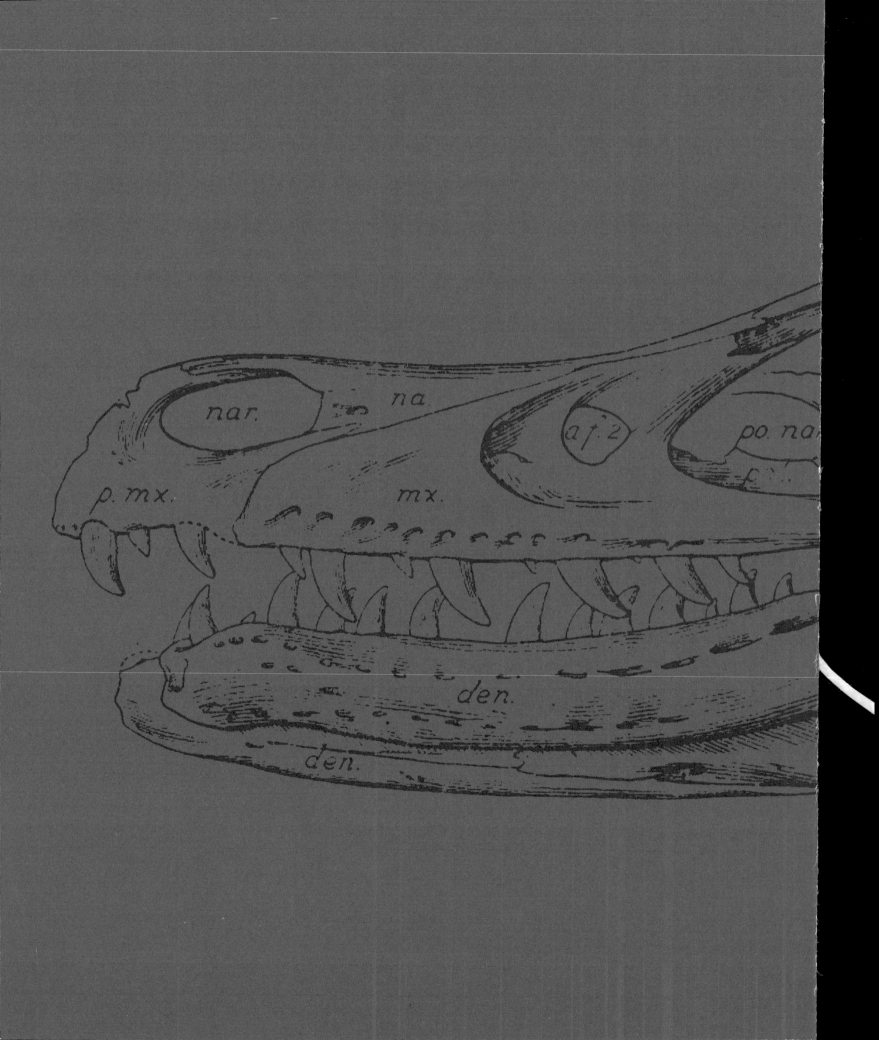